Bonjour et bienvenue!

My Weekly French Journal belongs to

....

French language Level.......................

Also by Anchal Verma

Littérature Fantastique Belge et Belgitude: Étude des nouvelles fantastiques de Jean Ray

My French Notebook: Ruled 6 sections Notebook/Diary with some useful French expressions

My Language Notebook: Ruled 6 sections Notebook with some useful expressions in different languages

French Vocabulary Bank: English-French bilingual vocabulary book of essential French words and phrases

This is my family C'est ma famille: A bilingual English French children's colourful family photo book and beginner book for learning French

For more information about Anchal Verma and her books, visit her website at https://anchalverma.com/

How to use My Weekly French Journal?

My weekly French journal is a 52-week (1 year) journal. For every week, there are two pages. The first is **My Goals** page, for you to write down your language learning goals for each day of the week. You can also specify here what language resources you plan to use every day for improving each skill. The second is **Week's Learnings** page, for you to reflect over the goals achieved or not yet achieved, during the week. Here there's also a note-taking space where you can jot down key points that you want to remember. This journal includes plenty of bonus material, which I hope would make learning French even more interesting for you.

Have fun learning French!

Les salutations (The greetings)

French	English
Salut	Hi
Bonjour	Hello, good morning
Bonsoir	Good evening
Bonne nuit	Goodnight
Ça va? (informal)	How are you?
Comment vas-tu? (informal)	How are you?
Comment allez-vous? (formal)	How are you?
Bien, merci	Good/Fine thank you
Pas mal	Not bad
Pas bien	Not well
Comme ci, comme ça	Ok/so so
Au revoir	Goodbye
Merci	Thank you
De rien	You are welcome
Et toi? (informal)	And you?
Et vous? (formal)	And you?

Vouloir, c'est pouvoir.
Where's there's a will,
there's a way.

My Goals

Week 1: / / to / /

Resources to use: Books/Dictionaries/Language Apps/Online sites...

Days of Week	Language Skills: Reading/Listening/Speaking/Writing/ Grammar
Monday:	
Tuesday:	
Wednesday:	
Thursday:	
Friday:	
Saturday/Sunday:	

Week's learnings

Week 1: / / to / /

Total hours allotted per week:

Goals reached:

Goals not yet reached:

Notes:

My Goals

Week 2: / / to / /

Resources to use: Books/Dictionaries/Language Apps/Online sites...

Days of Week	Language Skills: Reading/Listening/Speaking/Writing/ Grammar
Monday:	
Tuesday:	
Wednesday:	
Thursday:	
Friday:	
Saturday/Sunday:	

Week's learnings

Week 2: / / to / /

Total hours allotted per week:

Goals reached:

Goals not yet reached:

Notes:

My Goals

Week 3: / / to / /

Resources to use: Books/Dictionaries/Language Apps/Online sites...

Days of Week	Language Skills: Reading/Listening/Speaking/Writing/ Grammar
Monday:	
Tuesday:	
Wednesday:	
Thursday:	
Friday:	
Saturday/Sunday:	

Week's learnings

Week 3: / / to / /

Total hours allotted per week:

Goals reached:

Goals not yet reached:

Notes:

My Goals

Week 4: / / to / /

Resources to use: Books/Dictionaries/Language Apps/Online sites...

Days of Week	Language Skills: Reading/Listening/Speaking/Writing/ Grammar
Monday:	
Tuesday:	
Wednesday:	
Thursday:	
Friday:	
Saturday/Sunday:	

Week's learnings

Week 4: / / to / /

Total hours allotted per week:

Goals reached:

Goals not yet reached:

Notes:

L'alphabet français (The French alphabet)

A	ah
B	beh
C	seh
D	deh
E	uh
F	eff
G	jay
H	aash
I	ee
J	zhee
K	kah
L	ell
M	em
N	en
O	oh
P	peh
Q	coo
R	air
S	ess
T	teh
U	ooh
V	veh
W	doobl-veh
X	eeks
Y	ee-grek
Z	zed

Qui n'avance pas, recule.
Who does not move
forward, recedes.

My Goals

Week 5: / / to / /

Resources to use: Books/Dictionaries/Language Apps/Online sites...

Days of Week	Language Skills: Reading/Listening/Speaking/Writing/ Grammar
Monday:	
Tuesday:	
Wednesday:	
Thursday:	
Friday:	
Saturday/Sunday:	

Week's learnings

Week 5: / / to / /

Total hours allotted per week:

Goals reached:

Goals not yet reached:

Notes:

My Goals

Week 6: / / to / /

Resources to use: Books/Dictionaries/Language Apps/Online sites...

Days of Week	Language Skills: Reading/Listening/Speaking/Writing/ Grammar
Monday:	
Tuesday:	
Wednesday:	
Thursday:	
Friday:	
Saturday/Sunday:	

Week's learnings

Week 6: / / to / /

Total hours allotted per week:

Goals reached:

Goals not yet reached:

Notes:

My Goals

Week 7: / / to / /

Resources to use: Books/Dictionaries/Language Apps/Online sites...

Days of Week	Language Skills: Reading/Listening/Speaking/Writing/ Grammar
Monday:	
Tuesday:	
Wednesday:	
Thursday:	
Friday:	
Saturday/Sunday:	

Week's learnings

Week 7:   / /   to   / /

Total hours allotted per week:

Goals reached:

Goals not yet reached:

Notes:

My Goals

Week 8: / / to / /

Resources to use: Books/Dictionaries/Language Apps/Online sites...

Days of Week	Language Skills: Reading/Listening/Speaking/Writing/ Grammar
Monday:	
Tuesday:	
Wednesday:	
Thursday:	
Friday:	
Saturday/Sunday:	

Week's learnings

Week 8: / / to / /

Total hours allotted per week:

Goals reached:

Goals not yet reached:

Notes:

Le temps (The weather)

Il fait quel temps dehors ? - How's the weather ?

Il fait beau - It's nice outside

Il fait mauvais – The weather's bad

Il fait chaud - It's hot

Il fait froid - It's cold

Il fait frais - It's cool

Il fait nuageux - It's cloudy

Il pleut - It's raining

Il neige - It's snowing

Il gèle - It's freezing

Il y a du soleil- Its sunny

Il y a du vent - It's windy

Il y a du brouillard - It's foggy

C'est en forgeant qu'on devient forgeron.
Practice makes perfect.

My Goals

Week 9: / / to / /

Resources to use: Books/Dictionaries/Language Apps/Online sites...

Days of Week	Language Skills: Reading/Listening/Speaking/Writing/ Grammar
Monday:	
Tuesday:	
Wednesday:	
Thursday:	
Friday:	
Saturday/Sunday:	

Week's learnings

Week 9: / / to / /

Total hours allotted per week:

Goals reached:

Goals not yet reached:

Notes:

My Goals

Week 10: / / to / /

Resources to use: Books/Dictionaries/Language Apps/Online sites...

Days of Week	Language Skills: Reading/Listening/Speaking/Writing/ Grammar
Monday:	
Tuesday:	
Wednesday:	
Thursday:	
Friday:	
Saturday/Sunday:	

Week's learnings

Week 10: / / to / /

Total hours allotted per week:

Goals reached:

Goals not yet reached:

Notes:

My Goals

Week 11: / / to / /

Resources to use: Books/Dictionaries/Language Apps/Online sites...

Days of Week	Language Skills: Reading/Listening/Speaking/Writing/ Grammar
Monday:	
Tuesday:	
Wednesday:	
Thursday:	
Friday:	
Saturday/Sunday:	

Week's learnings

Week 11: / / to / /

Total hours allotted per week:

Goals reached:

Goals not yet reached:

Notes:

My Goals

Week 12: / / to / /

Resources to use: Books/Dictionaries/Language Apps/Online sites...

Days of Week	Language Skills: Reading/Listening/Speaking/Writing/ Grammar
Monday:	
Tuesday:	
Wednesday:	
Thursday:	
Friday:	
Saturday/Sunday:	

Week's learnings

Week 12: / / to / /

Total hours allotted per week:

Goals reached:

Goals not yet reached:

Notes:

Did you know?

France is the producer of more than 500 different types of cheese.

Après la pluie le beau temps.

Every cloud has a silver lining.

My Goals

Week 13: / / to / /

Resources to use: Books/Dictionaries/Language Apps/Online sites...

Days of Week	Language Skills: Reading/Listening/Speaking/Writing/ Grammar
Monday:	
Tuesday:	
Wednesday:	
Thursday:	
Friday:	
Saturday/Sunday:	

Week's learnings

Week 13: / / to / /

Total hours allotted per week:

Goals reached:

Goals not yet reached:

Notes:

My Goals

Week 14: / / to / /

Resources to use: Books/Dictionaries/Language Apps/Online sites...

Days of Week	Language Skills: Reading/Listening/Speaking/Writing/ Grammar
Monday:	
Tuesday:	
Wednesday:	
Thursday:	
Friday:	
Saturday/Sunday:	

Week's learnings

Week 14: / / to / /

Total hours allotted per week:

Goals reached:

Goals not yet reached:

Notes:

My Goals

Week 15: / / to / /

Resources to use: Books/Dictionaries/Language Apps/Online sites...

Days of Week	Language Skills: Reading/Listening/Speaking/Writing/ Grammar
Monday:	
Tuesday:	
Wednesday:	
Thursday:	
Friday:	
Saturday/Sunday:	

Week's learnings

Week 15: / / to / /

Total hours allotted per week:

Goals reached:

Goals not yet reached:

Notes:

My Goals

Week 16: / / to / /

Resources to use: Books/Dictionaries/Language Apps/Online sites...

Days of Week	Language Skills: Reading/Listening/Speaking/Writing/ Grammar
Monday:	
Tuesday:	
Wednesday:	
Thursday:	
Friday:	
Saturday/Sunday:	

Week's learnings

Week 16: / / to / /

Total hours allotted per week:

Goals reached:

Goals not yet reached:

Notes:

Les numéros 1-20 (Numbers 1-20)

French	English	Pronunciation
Zéro	Zero	Zay-roh
Un	One	Ahn
Deux	Two	Deuh
Trois	Three	Twah
Quatre	Four	Katr
Cinq	Five	Sank
Six	Six	Seess
Sept	Seven	Set
Huit	Eight	weet
Neuf	Nine	Nuf
Dix	Ten	Deess
Onze	Eleven	Onz
Douze	Twelve	Dooz
Treize	Thirteen	Trez
Quatorze	Fourteen	Kat-orz
Quinze	Fifteen	Kanz
Seize	Sixteen	Sez
Dix-sept	Seventeen	Dees-set
Dix-huit	Eighteen	Dees-weet
Dix-neuf	Nineteen	Dees-nuf
Vingt	Twenty	Van

L'habit ne fait pas le moine.

Don't judge a person by their appearance.

My Goals

Week 17: / / to / /

Resources to use: Books/Dictionaries/Language Apps/Online sites...

Days of Week	Language Skills: Reading/Listening/Speaking/Writing/ Grammar
Monday:	
Tuesday:	
Wednesday:	
Thursday:	
Friday:	
Saturday/Sunday:	

Week's learnings

Week 17: / / to / /

Total hours allotted per week:

Goals reached:

Goals not yet reached:

Notes:

My Goals

Week 18: / / to / /

Resources to use: Books/Dictionaries/Language Apps/Online sites...

Days of Week	Language Skills: Reading/Listening/Speaking/Writing/ Grammar
Monday:	
Tuesday:	
Wednesday:	
Thursday:	
Friday:	
Saturday/Sunday:	

Week's learnings

Week 18: / / to / /

Total hours allotted per week:

Goals reached:

Goals not yet reached:

Notes:

My Goals

Week 19: / / to / /

Resources to use: Books/Dictionaries/Language Apps/Online sites...

Days of Week	Language Skills: Reading/Listening/Speaking/Writing/ Grammar
Monday:	
Tuesday:	
Wednesday:	
Thursday:	
Friday:	
Saturday/Sunday:	

Week's learnings

Week 19: / / to / /

Total hours allotted per week:

Goals reached:

Goals not yet reached:

Notes:

My Goals

Week 20: / / to / /

Resources to use: Books/Dictionaries/Language Apps/Online sites...

Days of Week	Language Skills: Reading/Listening/Speaking/Writing/ Grammar
Monday:	
Tuesday:	
Wednesday:	
Thursday:	
Friday:	
Saturday/Sunday:	

Week's learnings

Week 20: / / to / /

Total hours allotted per week:

Goals reached:

Goals not yet reached:

Notes:

COULEURS

COLORS

French	English
Bleu	Blue
Rouge	Red
Jaune	Yellow
Vert	Green
Noir	Black
Marron	Brown
Orange	Orange
Violet	Purple
Gris	Grey
Blanc	White

Il ne faut jamais dire : Fontaine, je ne boirai pas de ton eau !

Never say never.

My Goals

Week 21: / / to / /

Resources to use: Books/Dictionaries/Language Apps/Online sites...

Days of Week	Language Skills: Reading/Listening/Speaking/Writing/ Grammar
Monday:	
Tuesday:	
Wednesday:	
Thursday:	
Friday:	
Saturday/Sunday:	

Week's learnings

Week 21: / / to / /

Total hours allotted per week:

Goals reached:

Goals not yet reached:

Notes:

My Goals

Week 22: / / to / /

Resources to use: Books/Dictionaries/Language Apps/Online sites...

Days of Week	Language Skills: Reading/Listening/Speaking/Writing/ Grammar
Monday:	
Tuesday:	
Wednesday:	
Thursday:	
Friday:	
Saturday/Sunday:	

Week's learnings

Week 22: / / to / /

Total hours allotted per week:

Goals reached:

Goals not yet reached:

Notes:

My Goals

Week 23: / / to / /

Resources to use: Books/Dictionaries/Language Apps/Online sites...

Days of Week	Language Skills: Reading/Listening/Speaking/Writing/ Grammar
Monday:	
Tuesday:	
Wednesday:	
Thursday:	
Friday:	
Saturday/Sunday:	

Week's learnings

Week 23: / / to / /

Total hours allotted per week:

Goals reached:

Goals not yet reached:

Notes:

My Goals

Week 24: / / to / /

Resources to use: Books/Dictionaries/Language Apps/Online sites...

Days of Week	Language Skills: Reading/Listening/Speaking/Writing/ Grammar
Monday:	
Tuesday:	
Wednesday:	
Thursday:	
Friday:	
Saturday/Sunday:	

Week's learnings

Week 24: / / to / /

Total hours allotted per week:

Goals reached:

Goals not yet reached:

Notes:

Did you know?

The national motto of France is Liberté, Egalité, Fraternité. (Liberty, Equality, Fraternity.)

Si jeunesse savait, si vieillesse pouvait.

If youth knew, if the elderly could.

My Goals

Week 25: / / to / /

Resources to use: Books/Dictionaries/Language Apps/Online sites...

Days of Week	Language Skills: Reading/Listening/Speaking/Writing/ Grammar
Monday:	
Tuesday:	
Wednesday:	
Thursday:	
Friday:	
Saturday/Sunday:	

Week's learnings

Week 25: / / to / /

Total hours allotted per week:

Goals reached:

Goals not yet reached:

Notes:

My Goals

Week 26: / / to / /

Resources to use: Books/Dictionaries/Language Apps/Online sites...

Days of Week	Language Skills: Reading/Listening/Speaking/Writing/ Grammar
Monday:	
Tuesday:	
Wednesday:	
Thursday:	
Friday:	
Saturday/Sunday:	

Week's learnings

Week 26: / / to / /

Total hours allotted per week:

Goals reached:

Goals not yet reached:

Notes:

My Goals

Week 27: / / to / /

Resources to use: Books/Dictionaries/Language Apps/Online sites...

Days of Week	Language Skills: Reading/Listening/Speaking/Writing/ Grammar
Monday:	
Tuesday:	
Wednesday:	
Thursday:	
Friday:	
Saturday/Sunday:	

Week's learnings

Week 27: / / to / /

Total hours allotted per week:

Goals reached:

Goals not yet reached:

Notes:

My Goals

Week 28: / / to / /

Resources to use: Books/Dictionaries/Language Apps/Online sites...

Days of Week	Language Skills: Reading/Listening/Speaking/Writing/ Grammar
Monday:	
Tuesday:	
Wednesday:	
Thursday:	
Friday:	
Saturday/Sunday:	

Week's learnings

Week 28: / / to / /

Total hours allotted per week:

Goals reached:

Goals not yet reached:

Notes:

Jours de la semaine (Days of the Week)

Lundi	Monday
Mardi	Tuesday
Mercredi	Wednesday
Jeudi	Thursday
Vendredi	Friday
Samedi	Saturday
Dimanche	Sunday

Mois de l'année (Months of the Year)

Janvier	January
Février	February
Mars	March
Avril	April
Mai	May
Juin	June
Juillet	July
Août	August
Septembre	September
Octobre	October
Novembre	November
Décembre	December

Il faut casser le noyau
pour avoir l'amande.

No pain no gain.

My Goals

Week 29: / / to / /

Resources to use: Books/Dictionaries/Language Apps/Online sites...

Days of Week	Language Skills: Reading/Listening/Speaking/Writing/ Grammar
Monday:	
Tuesday:	
Wednesday:	
Thursday:	
Friday:	
Saturday/Sunday:	

Week's learnings

Week 29: / / to / /

Total hours allotted per week:

Goals reached:

Goals not yet reached:

Notes:

My Goals

Week 30: / / to / /

Resources to use: Books/Dictionaries/Language Apps/Online sites...

Days of Week	Language Skills: Reading/Listening/Speaking/Writing/ Grammar
Monday:	
Tuesday:	
Wednesday:	
Thursday:	
Friday:	
Saturday/Sunday:	

Week's learnings

Week 30: / / to / /

Total hours allotted per week:

Goals reached:

Goals not yet reached:

Notes:

My Goals

Week 31: / / to / /

Resources to use: Books/Dictionaries/Language Apps/Online sites...

Days of Week	Language Skills: Reading/Listening/Speaking/Writing/ Grammar
Monday:	
Tuesday:	
Wednesday:	
Thursday:	
Friday:	
Saturday/Sunday:	

Week's learnings

Week 31: / / to / /

Total hours allotted per week:

Goals reached:

Goals not yet reached:

Notes:

My Goals

Week 32: / / to / /

Resources to use: Books/Dictionaries/Language Apps/Online sites...

Days of Week	Language Skills: Reading/Listening/Speaking/Writing/ Grammar
Monday:	
Tuesday:	
Wednesday:	
Thursday:	
Friday:	
Saturday/Sunday:	

Week's learnings

Week 32: / / to / /

Total hours allotted per week:

Goals reached:

Goals not yet reached:

Notes:

Quelques expressions françaises utiles
(Some useful French expressions)

Expression française (French expression)	Traduction en anglais (Translation in English)
Comment tu t'appelles? (informal)	What is your name?
Comment vous appelez-vous? (formal)	What is your name?
Je m'appelle	My name is
Désolé(e)	Sorry
Je ne sais pas	I don't know
Je ne comprend pas	I don't understand
S'il te plaît (informal)	Please
S'il vous plaît (formal)	Please
C'est tout	That's it
Répétez, s'il vous plaît!	Please repeat
Je suis	I am
J'ai	I have
Oui	Yes
Non	No
C'est quelle page ?	Which page is it ?
Pouvez-vous m'aider ?	Could you help me?

Impossible n'est pas français.

Nothing is impossible.

My Goals

Week 33: / / to / /

Resources to use: Books/Dictionaries/Language Apps/Online sites...

Days of Week	Language Skills: Reading/Listening/Speaking/Writing/ Grammar
Monday:	
Tuesday:	
Wednesday:	
Thursday:	
Friday:	
Saturday/Sunday:	

Week's learnings

Week 33: / / to / /

Total hours allotted per week:

Goals reached:

Goals not yet reached:

Notes:

My Goals

Week 34: / / to / /

Resources to use: Books/Dictionaries/Language Apps/Online sites...

Days of Week	Language Skills: Reading/Listening/Speaking/Writing/ Grammar
Monday:	
Tuesday:	
Wednesday:	
Thursday:	
Friday:	
Saturday/Sunday:	

Week's learnings

Week 34: / / to / /

Total hours allotted per week:

Goals reached:

Goals not yet reached:

Notes:

My Goals

Week 35: / / to / /

Resources to use: Books/Dictionaries/Language Apps/Online sites...

Days of Week	Language Skills: Reading/Listening/Speaking/Writing/ Grammar
Monday:	
Tuesday:	
Wednesday:	
Thursday:	
Friday:	
Saturday/Sunday:	

Week's learnings

Week 35: / / to / /

Total hours allotted per week:

Goals reached:

Goals not yet reached:

Notes:

My Goals

Week 36: / / to / /

Resources to use: Books/Dictionaries/Language Apps/Online sites...

Days of Week	Language Skills: Reading/Listening/Speaking/Writing/ Grammar
Monday:	
Tuesday:	
Wednesday:	
Thursday:	
Friday:	
Saturday/Sunday:	

Week's learnings

Week 36: / / to / /

Total hours allotted per week:

Goals reached:

Goals not yet reached:

Notes:

Did you know?

French is an official working language of several organisations like United Nations, NATO, and the International Olympic Committee.

Petit à petit, l'oiseau fait son nid.

Slow and steady wins the race.

My Goals

Week 37: / / to / /

Resources to use: Books/Dictionaries/Language Apps/Online sites...

Days of Week	Language Skills: Reading/Listening/Speaking/Writing/ Grammar
Monday:	
Tuesday:	
Wednesday:	
Thursday:	
Friday:	
Saturday/Sunday:	

Week's learnings

Week 37: / / to / /

Total hours allotted per week:

Goals reached:

Goals not yet reached:

Notes:

My Goals

Week 38: / / to / /

Resources to use: Books/Dictionaries/Language Apps/Online sites...

Days of Week	Language Skills: Reading/Listening/Speaking/Writing/ Grammar
Monday:	
Tuesday:	
Wednesday:	
Thursday:	
Friday:	
Saturday/Sunday:	

Week's learnings

Week 38: / / to / /

Total hours allotted per week:

Goals reached:

Goals not yet reached:

Notes:

My Goals

Week 39: / / to / /

Resources to use: Books/Dictionaries/Language Apps/Online sites...

Days of Week	Language Skills: Reading/Listening/Speaking/Writing/ Grammar
Monday:	
Tuesday:	
Wednesday:	
Thursday:	
Friday:	
Saturday/Sunday:	

Week's learnings

Week 39: / / to / /

Total hours allotted per week:

Goals reached:

Goals not yet reached:

Notes:

My Goals

Week 40: / / to / /

Resources to use: Books/Dictionaries/Language Apps/Online sites...

Days of Week	Language Skills: Reading/Listening/Speaking/Writing/ Grammar
Monday:	
Tuesday:	
Wednesday:	
Thursday:	
Friday:	
Saturday/Sunday:	

Week's learnings

Week 40: / / to / /

Total hours allotted per week:

Goals reached:

Goals not yet reached:

Notes:

La Conjugaison des verbes
(The verb conjugation)

Les verbes en -er

Habiter= to live	
J'	habite
Tu	habites
Il/Elle	habite
Nous	habitons
Vous	habitez
Ils/Elles	habitent

Travailler = to work	
Je	travaille
Tu	travailles
Il/Elle	travaille
Nous	travaillons
Vous	travaillez
Ils/Elles	travaillent

Les verbes en -ir et en -re

Lire= to read	
Je	lis
Tu	lis
Il/Elle	lit
Nous	lisons
Vous	lisez
Ils/Elles	lisent

Choisir= to choose	
Je	choisis
Tu	choisis
Il/Elle	choisit
Nous	choisissons
Vous	choisissez
Ils/Elles	choisissent

À vous maintenant ! (It's your turn now!)

Détester=to hate
Je …………
Tu…………
Il/Elle………
Nous……….
Vous……….
Ils/Elles…….

Finir = to finish
Je …………
Tu…………
Il/Elle………
Nous……….
Vous……….
Ils/Elles…….

Mieux vaut tard que jamais.

Better late than never.

My Goals

Week 41: / / to / /

Resources to use: Books/Dictionaries/Language Apps/Online sites...

Days of Week	Language Skills: Reading/Listening/Speaking/Writing/ Grammar
Monday:	
Tuesday:	
Wednesday:	
Thursday:	
Friday:	
Saturday/Sunday:	

Week's learnings

Week 41: / / to / /

Total hours allotted per week:

Goals reached:

Goals not yet reached:

Notes:

My Goals

Week 42: / / to / /

Resources to use: Books/Dictionaries/Language Apps/Online sites...

Days of Week	Language Skills: Reading/Listening/Speaking/Writing/ Grammar
Monday:	
Tuesday:	
Wednesday:	
Thursday:	
Friday:	
Saturday/Sunday:	

Week's learnings

Week 42: / / to / /

Total hours allotted per week:

Goals reached:

Goals not yet reached:

Notes:

My Goals

Week 43: / / to / /

Resources to use: Books/Dictionaries/Language Apps/Online sites...

Days of Week	Language Skills: Reading/Listening/Speaking/Writing/ Grammar
Monday:	
Tuesday:	
Wednesday:	
Thursday:	
Friday:	
Saturday/Sunday:	

Week's learnings

Week 43: / / to / /

Total hours allotted per week:

Goals reached:

Goals not yet reached:

Notes:

My Goals

Week 44: / / to / /

Resources to use: Books/Dictionaries/Language Apps/Online sites...

Days of Week	Language Skills: Reading/Listening/Speaking/Writing/ Grammar
Monday:	
Tuesday:	
Wednesday:	
Thursday:	
Friday:	
Saturday/Sunday:	

Week's learnings

Week 44: / / to / /

Total hours allotted per week:

Goals reached:

Goals not yet reached:

Notes:

Les verbes français les plus répandus (The most common French Verbs)

French	English
Parler	To speak
Aimer	To love
Détester	To hate
Travailler	To work
Écouter	To listen
Venir	To come
Aller	To go
Être	To be
Avoir	To have
Demander	To ask
Écrire	To write
Lire	To read
Dire	To say
Sortir	To go out
Donner	To give
Penser	To think
Regarder	To watch
Répondre	To answer
Ouvrir	To open

Tout est bien qui finit bien.

All's well that ends well.

My Goals

Week 45:   / /   to   / /

Resources to use: Books/Dictionaries/Language Apps/Online sites...

Days of Week	Language Skills: Reading/Listening/Speaking/Writing/ Grammar
Monday:	
Tuesday:	
Wednesday:	
Thursday:	
Friday:	
Saturday/Sunday:	

Week's learnings

Week 45: / / to / /

Total hours allotted per week:

Goals reached:

Goals not yet reached:

Notes:

My Goals

Week 46: / / to / /

Resources to use: Books/Dictionaries/Language Apps/Online sites...

Days of Week	Language Skills: Reading/Listening/Speaking/Writing/ Grammar
Monday:	
Tuesday:	
Wednesday:	
Thursday:	
Friday:	
Saturday/Sunday:	

Week's learnings

Week 46: / / to / /

Total hours allotted per week:

Goals reached:

Goals not yet reached:

Notes:

My Goals

Week 47: / / to / /

Resources to use: Books/Dictionaries/Language Apps/Online sites...

Days of Week	Language Skills: Reading/Listening/Speaking/Writing/ Grammar
Monday:	
Tuesday:	
Wednesday:	
Thursday:	
Friday:	
Saturday/Sunday:	

Week's learnings

Week 47: / / to / /

Total hours allotted per week:

Goals reached:

Goals not yet reached:

Notes:

My Goals

Week 48: / / to / /

Resources to use: Books/Dictionaries/Language Apps/Online sites...

Days of Week	Language Skills: Reading/Listening/Speaking/Writing/ Grammar
Monday:	
Tuesday:	
Wednesday:	
Thursday:	
Friday:	
Saturday/Sunday:	

Week's learnings

Week 48: / / to / /

Total hours allotted per week:

Goals reached:

Goals not yet reached:

Notes:

Des virelangues français (French tongue twisters)

- *Cinq chiens chassent six chats. (Five dogs hunt six cats.)*
- *Lily lit le livre dans le lit. (Lily reads the book in the bed.)*
- *Seize chaises sèchent. (Sixteen chairs are drying.)*
- *La mule a bu tant qu'elle a pu. (The mule drank all that it could.)*
- *Dans ta tente ta tante t'attend. (Your aunt is waiting for you in your tent.)*
- *Poisson sans boisson est poison. (Fish without drink is poison.)*
- *Un chasseur sachant chasser chasse sans son chien. (A hunter who knows how to hunt hunts without his dog.)*
- *Si mon tonton tond ton tonton, ton tonton sera tondu. – If my uncle shaves your uncle, your uncle will be shaved.*
- *Le ver vert va vers le verre vert.* (The green worm goes toward the green glass.)
- *Je suis ce que je suis, et si je suis ce que je suis, qu'est-ce que je suis ? (I am what I am, and if I am what I am, what am I ?)*

Did you know?

The first cell
phone camera
was invented in
France by
Philippe Kahn
in 1997.

My Goals

Week 49: / / to / /

Resources to use: Books/Dictionaries/Language Apps/Online sites...

Days of Week	Language Skills: Reading/Listening/Speaking/Writing/ Grammar
Monday:	
Tuesday:	
Wednesday:	
Thursday:	
Friday:	
Saturday/Sunday:	

Week's learnings

Week 49: / / to / /

Total hours allotted per week:

Goals reached:

Goals not yet reached:

Notes:

My Goals

Week 50: / / to / /

Resources to use: Books/Dictionaries/Language Apps/Online sites...

Days of Week	Language Skills: Reading/Listening/Speaking/Writing/ Grammar
Monday:	
Tuesday:	
Wednesday:	
Thursday:	
Friday:	
Saturday/Sunday:	

Week's learnings

Week 50: / / to / /

Total hours allotted per week:

Goals reached:

Goals not yet reached:

Notes:

My Goals

Week 51: / / to / /

Resources to use: Books/Dictionaries/Language Apps/Online sites...

Days of Week	Language Skills: Reading/Listening/Speaking/Writing/ Grammar
Monday:	
Tuesday:	
Wednesday:	
Thursday:	
Friday:	
Saturday/Sunday:	

Week's learnings

Week 51: / / to / /

Total hours allotted per week:

Goals reached:

Goals not yet reached:

Notes:

My Goals

Week 52: / / to / /

Resources to use: Books/Dictionaries/Language Apps/Online sites...

Days of Week	Language Skills: Reading/Listening/Speaking/Writing/ Grammar
Monday:	
Tuesday:	
Wednesday:	
Thursday:	
Friday:	
Saturday/Sunday:	

Week's learnings

Week 52: / / to / /

Total hours allotted per week:

Goals reached:

Goals not yet reached:

Notes:

Printed at Repro India Ltd.